The L

Maurice Whelan

The Lilac Bow

Poems & Prose

Acknowledgements

'A Journey Through Time' was first published in
The Kildare Nationalist 25 February 2005.

I am grateful to countless people who have taken the time over the
past few years to read my poems. I am particularly indebted to the
following: Lena Bruselid, Gary Bryson, Michael Dudley,
Judy Griffiths, Winton Higgins, Louise Newman,
Richard O'Neill-Dean, Tania Perich, Stuart Rees, Lorraine Rose,
Bob Stern, Ella Whelan, Louise Whelan, Bob White.
Their comments and criticisms have improved my writing;
its failings are my own.
My thanks to Stephen Matthews for publishing my work.

GINNINDERRA PRESS

PO Box 3461 Port Adelaide SA 5015
www.ginninderrapress.com.au

Contents

Dedication

to Anthony
in whose presence
the wondrous words
of the poets
of Yeats and Keats
and Shakespeare
first found wings

'There is a method of trying periods on the ear, or weighing them with the scales of the breath, without any articulate sound. Authors, as they write, may be said to hear a sound so fine, there's nothing lives 'twixt it and silence.'

William Hazlitt, *On the Conversation of Authors*

High Flyer

Soaring on wings
high above the escarpment
circling

while the hourglass builds
a small mountain
of sand

How long has it been?

How long has it been? Is it ten years?
Twelve if it's been a day!
You're looking good, he said to me.
The man beside him caught my eye,
raised his bottle of beer
and moved away.
You haven't changed a bit, I said.
He changed his grip on his dripping wine glass
and offered a limp handshake

The same small eyes peered over the parapets
lost in each stroke of the present time.
Nothing had been ventured,
the future always took his breath away,
a deep chasm waiting to devour him,
the past a mine of dreams
never explored.

The man with the bottle of beer returned
and caught my eye.
I could see he knew more
than when last he looked my way.

Sea Creatures

Shoals of memories
Moments of our past
Swim the oceans of our lives

We who are wanderers
Mingle with the currents

You that stand
Feet firm upon the shore
Cast the nets

Muscae Volitantes

In memoriam John McGahern

Staring into the middle distance
seeing nothing
lost in half a thought
signalled its entrance.
It came from south by south-west
and moved slowly upwards
towards the centre of things.
It never arrived at its destination
and disappeared
without trace or trail
from the radar of my eye.

Over the years
I grew familiar with its presence
and absence.
I drew attention to it
when a new pair of reading glasses was required.
She called it a floater – muscae volitantes
a Pluto moving mysteriously
alone
away in the far-out regions.

A lilac tree grew at the gable end of our home
beside the garage
and when possessed of abundance
it filled the air with perfumed delight.
A walk within the gravitational force of its affections
dispelled the farmyard odours of cow dung and diesel.

Peering upwards into its canopy of colour
lifted up my eyes from my six-year-old feet
that had stood on the engine oil
that seeped into the beaten
broken earth of the garage floor.

Staring into the middle distance
desiring nothing
my purple sun rises and descends
and cradles me within a waif-like stillness.
The compass of my heart
trembles and silent whispers
herald the approach
of a faint and distant fragrance.

Mistakes have taught me to quell my appetite.
I will not turn to see
or reach to touch
or strain for sound.
My body
like a musical instrument
has become attuned
and when the lilac bow draws slowly up
and down
and plays on the strings of all my senses,
I inhale incense from the heavens,
and soar
inside a single moment of eternity.

I will never look into your eyes

After London 7 July 2005

On the last night, sleep is far from me.
Distant sounds empty of all colour
Gather to announce my end.
I will never look into your eyes.

I dress for my last day.
I cover my body with the garment of death.
I pass the mirror in my room.
I will not look into my eyes.

I walk beside you into the waiting train.
I see you smile as you touch a hand
You will never touch again.
I cannot look into your eyes.

A father dries the tears of a crying child.
A baby drinking from his mother's breast
Turns to me.
I will not look into his eyes.

A girl in blue stands smiling,
In her hand the hallowed book.
I blow them all to blood and dust.
I will never look into her eyes.

They say I will be counted holy,
They promise a seat among the blessed,
But I have slain both young and old,
Stolen the life of a new-born child.
How will I look into His eyes?

Cogito, Ergo…

I think therefore I am
I think therefore I
I think therefore
I think
I

Phew!
That was close!

Child Overboard

With sombre face
you front the television camera
and speak of a terrible tragedy,
a small child in a suburban
backyard pool drowned.
You extend condolences and with faltering voice
say on behalf of the government
your heart and the hearts of all Australians
go out to the parents and family
at this time of unspeakable loss and grief.

Why were you so swift to say
I threw my son to the raging sea?
Why did your heart believe
that I was heartless?

Gather your sorrow and the pain
that has touched your life,
place it upon the scales,
weigh it next to mine.

My daughter – still a child – raped,
my husband's hacked and beaten body
dumped on my threshold.
In dead of night I steal away,
walk for weeks under a blistering sun,
part with all that I possessed,
receive passage on a craft,
a coffin ship that sought to claim our lives.

I have lost my home my husband,
my country, the cradle of my life.

Gather your sorrow and your pain,
place it all upon the scales,
weigh it next to mine.

Still Life

(Blue Mountains, NSW)

Without the silence and solitude
amidst this ocean of greens and blues,
trees and skies,
that wraps itself round me
when I'm still,
enfolds me in its arms
and offers a fathomless freedom
to look and breathe and think,
without it I fear
I'd shrink and shrivel
and lose the zest for life.

Fancy Dresser

The cool water touched her feet and retreated
into the white wet sands. The pale pink morning
sky stretched from the sea's horizon beyond her.

She had slept naked in her wooden cabin, rose and walked
alone to greet the waves. Her flesh tingled as rays
of hope reached down from the edge of the firmament

and danced upon the surface of her sparkling skin.
The wind kissed the nape of her slender neck
and the smell of sea salt sweetened the air,

love embraced and entered her and a veil of pink
translucent light settled softly upon the silent
surface of her body like a pale silk gown.

It came last night

It came last night between the folds of my sleep
and now I await its return.
Large raindrops fall softly on tin roof,
jacaranda leaves overflow and let fall.
In silence I listen.

It will seep into me when I take a breath,
when it goes deep and deeper and
when at last I release all hold.

Archimedes, it is said,
pushed his brain to the limit
to solve the riddle of the king's gold crown
but only when he ceased his thoughts,
when he put aside the labour of the day,
when he stepped into his warm bath,
when his body felt its own buoyancy,
only then did he know and he was free
to shout his naked Eureka.

All my life I have furrowed my brow
stretched the sinews of my brain
to breaking point.
Last night a truth came inside my sleep,
unheralded,
unexpected,
just dropping in,
nature acknowledged for what it is,
accepting and accepted,
floating in the tissue of a dream,
gently warming
and most, most welcome.

Fire

7 February 2009 Victoria Australia

Waves
of fire
like a tsunami
sweep over the land
the tops of tall trees
like seaweed
bob on the surface
of the burning ocean.

Searing currents consume
every thing that stands
upon the ground
homes plants cars men
women children and the old
felled by the merciless flame.

We the living
wander amidst
grey-white ashen ruins
of half-lived lives
eyes smarting
lungs tightening.

With scorched spirits
where shall we find strength
for tears?

Enchanted

As a boy growing up in Ireland, this island was a place in some remote corner of the world and possessed a name to conjure with – Van Diemen's Land. To a child's ear its sound rang out its sense - the abode of demons! To its far-flung and inhospitable shores the cream of Irish rebels and patriots had in the last century been banished. We were told it was a place of doubtful return, where the chains of seven or fourteen years' transportation meant certain death. But that was history. A new name had been conferred, and during the past twenty-five years its mountains, valleys, rivers and trees had become the showpiece of the movement to protect and preserve the gifts mankind has received from Nature.

I had lived for a decade on the mainland of Australia before the prospect of a trip to Tasmania presented itself. Friends had spoken of the place and their eyes light up as they re-lived their travels. 'Think big' was the motto. 'Wild spaces, great mountains, huge trees and vast rivers. You can trek for days through the wilderness without meeting a fellow human being!'

So it was a surprise that on the afternoon of the second day of my holiday I stood at the base of Cradle Mountain reading a sign which said, 'Enchanted Walk, twenty minutes return, 1.2 km circuit. Easy, gentle and mostly level.' I was geared up for greater things. However, the map of the route was simplicity itself. A diagram roughly in the shape of a rectangle provided an overview: start at the bridge; walk on the track along the left side of the stream; use the wooden footbridge to cross to the other side, and return along the right-hand bank. Child's play! I glanced at my watch and decided to start at once and knew I'd be back by teatime.

As I set out, tussocks of button grass with long slender golden-green leaves covered all the open ground to the left. They grow on what is really a bog, and if stricken by a forest fire are difficult to extinguish and can burn for months. No hint of such danger on this crisp day, no signs of underground smouldering. The stream which was some twenty metres to the right cannot be seen. Trees and shrubs grow plentiful along its bank and shield it from view. The occasional sounds of the stream running along mingle with the uneven rustling of the grass, and the shimmering of the leaves of the few alpine yellow gum trees dotted along the route. I had soon completed half of the walk without a hint of enchantment.

On the narrow footbridge the light changed. I looked up. Like fingers interlocking in an act of prayer, the topmost branches of the trees had joined together. They offered a portal into an unknown place. Halfway across the bridge I stalled; I was in another world. Although I knew I could retrieve my steps, it seemed as if a door had been closed. Only one way to go – forward through the narrow gate. It was like walking into a surprise party as the guest of honour. But here all was silent. No human hands to sound a welcome; no voices raised to cheer. Instead a greeting, which was as silent as it was still, startling in its simplicity. An all-pervading greenery to meet the eyes; a fruitful, dank smell to inhale; tree branches overladen with moss, lichen and old man's beard stretching out, inviting a handshake. I inhaled the cool, clean air.

Downstream, to my right, two large myrtle beech trees make an angled arch as they stand resting upon each other midstream. For a long time, perhaps hundreds of years, they had grown on either side of the stream. One might wonder how they came together and could fancy that, like long separated lovers, they at last broke loose from the bonds which bound them, a Juliet and her Romeo, falling into each other's arms across the great divide. But it was more likely one fell first and later the other, larger one, having been rested upon, eventually itself gave way. Now they stand in mutual support, uprooted but still living, their branches grown into a solid embrace. And when they come to fall, they will fall together.

Upstream, the flowing waters, brown with tannin, emerge out of an impenetrable mass of dense green foliage. Both banks are heavily populated and here too an arch has formed, with branches reaching out from each side, creating a tunnel through which the waters run. Everywhere there is green: all the tree trunks, branches and stems, and even the ground itself; everything is garmented in mosses and lichens.

Standing, watching, waiting within this verdurous world the light and colours grow soft. Slowly my eyes adapt and like a fine veil rising and dissolving, like a mist clearing, a multitude of spaces open up before me. It is like a secret garden with many points of entry, through which the eye can travel. I think of the old Raree-show, where you press your eye close to the small aperture and wait to see the world beyond. I remember the face of my son, when as a toddler on Christmas morning he unwrapped a kaleidoscope, and the awkward uncertainty of getting his eyes in the right place gave way and his whole face was filled with awe and wonder - a moment I will never forget.

Now, I am a child: my face filled with wonder; I can sense my cheeks glowing. Each small step I take each movement of my eyes and I am granted entry into another part of the forest's depths. I could stay here for hours, days.

Still standing on the bridge, the furthest point of view is no more than a stone's throw away, and yet it seems I am surrounded by a galaxy of life forms. In my mind's eye I retraced my steps to the foot of Cradle Mountain and Dove Lake where I had walked three hours earlier. I remember the vastness of the mountain itself and its reflection in the still water of the lake. People walked along the far distant peaks of the mountain range, like tiny moving specks. I thought of our place in this total landscape, our insignificance against the mass of this majestic mountain, its lofty peaks and the panorama of blue sky, upwards and beyond, stretching the eyes and the mind beyond their limits.

From childhood we hear of the enchanted wood as the home of a menacing presence, set to entrap and control us. I leave the bridge and wander along the path. The trees momentarily thin out and little patches of sunlight find their way in; there is evidence of wombats and wallabies. A truncated stump of a King Billy pine about two metres tall is witness to the fact that at some time past human saws had played a part in the shape of things. With a flat roof and a small opening at its base and a cloak of green laid upon it, I could imagine it as the home of fairies and elves.

All of a sudden, everything changed. My eyes, which had become accustomed to the soft, sweet light now turned towards a harsh whiteness. The canopy of the forest had been damaged and blinding light poured down. On the opposite bank a myrtle beech had recently fallen and it lay across the stream. It was like the scene of a road traffic accident—a car mounting a pavement and ploughing into a liner of pedestrians. Violence hung in the air. I could almost feel the earth below me tremble, could hear the crack of timber and the swish of branch and leaves hurtling

25

to the ground. The bank beside my feet where the top of the tree had landed was cracked and broken – I could reach down and place my fingers in the open wounds of the earth.

I look across at the upturned base and roots of the tree ripped from the soil; debris was scattered everywhere. A small shrub, an Archeria, which had rested in the shadow of the myrtle beech, had become collateral damage. It had been broken by the fall but was still standing; its raw, white, flesh pleaded for help and protection.

I stare at the mass of upturned roots and soil: I am a trespasser, a witness to a rapacious strike; intimate parts violently ripped from their privacy and shown to the world; the floor of the forest like the floor of an abattoir.

I turn away. I start to weep and as I dry my face with the backs of my hands suddenly I feel self-conscious - a grown man crying for a tree! Beside the path there is another large tree which had fallen many years ago, perhaps before I was born. While the top of the tree was clearly still visible, the base had sunk into the ground and a blanket of moss and lichen seamlessly joined soil and decaying wood, as if the earth was slowly receiving it back. 'Dust thou art and unto dust thou shalt return.' Whether it had been a timely fall fifty years ago I will never know, but since then it has lain upon the ground still, submitting itself to the laws of the forest, its task now changed – but forever remaining the same.

Do we gracefully surrender the life force we have borrowed? What do we all bequeath to others when we fall?

I move on and glance back at the recently fallen tree that has reduced me to tears. Soon, in nature's time the hole in the forest's roof would close, the light would soften, the raw wounds would heal, the scars on the body of the broken earth would level and settle and, like a new-born fabric, a cloak of luscious green would imperceptibly be woven and spread itself.

Last night I dreamt. I saw a man walking onto a bridge. I hid behind a tree. Other people passed by the man but he gave no sign of seeing them. I came out of hiding and offered to be his guide, but I too was invisible to him and he paid me no attention but when it moved on I saw him looking where I had been pointed. Then, like two clouds floating into each other and becoming one I slowly merged with him. I felt the wry smile on our face and I could hear the workings of our mind. A great net – like the safety-net trapeze artistes use – appeared and spread over the whole forest. Spun from finely woven silk it glistened like spiders' webs glisten in the early morning dew. 'We' became light and floated through the air unhindered by gravity. Then all the waters of the creek increased and formed a great waterfall and in its foam and spray we floated out of the forest. Outside, I was standing at the sign where the walk began. I was talking to someone who knew him well. He and I became one. She could read our eyes. Everything that had been seen was written there.

Dream Woman

In all her beautiful nakedness
she stepped beside him into the shower
her soft right hip and thigh
were all that his eyes were resting on
choose me she said
although she said nothing
her body and her presence spoke
she had stepped into a space
she just wanted to be there
he began to worry as sometime
sometime ago in a dream
yesterday it was
was it
that another had said
choose me
and he had
he touched the generous sleek thigh and hip
not now she said
restless
he grew restless
that she and her would rage
against the other
against him
two-timer
full of what he thinks he can get for nothing
full of deceit and weakness
a bob each way
then everything became opaque
iridescent
simmering

flickering
in the twilight of his mind
she
and her
were possessed of a great calm
a silent and serene peace
how could it be
how could all the worry
the fervent fretting
the pounding heart
belong to him
alone
she and her were devoid of desire
of lust
they did not crave
they just wanted to be
he could not understand
he wondered at it all
ever since he could remember
there was strife and fear
how is it possible
that woman could be one
that arms and thighs and breasts and lips
could hold such calm
could still the storm
in his raging mind
could be the proud possessors
of a single
silent
peace.

The Eternal Now

When

>I place a seashell upon your hand;
>stand at your side and stare at a yellow sunset;
>the moon paints our faces silver-white;
>
>I point to the pink hibiscus;
>say the tea has a hint of peppermint
>and you should try it;
>
>I want you to close your eyes
>listen to a Heaney poem
>a song by Joni Mitchell or Leonard Cohen;
>
>I take your hand and we walk in the bush
>inhale moist air overladen
>with sweet eucalyptus;

I see a moment of your birth, my child,
I meet a moment of my death, my child.

Sweet Freedom

And now, gentlemen, cast your eyes on this fine exhibit
and you will see that I have kept the best till last.
Where in the length and breath of these colonies

will you find such a fine beast of burden?
No, sir, I have a reputation to uphold.
Who's to start? What am I bid? Come, gentlemen,

step forward and see this fine head, these strong teeth,
this shining dark skin, feel these arms, these legs, ten pieces!
She's a steal at such a price, who will bid me more?

With whip in hand and arm extended, he pointed to the circle of twenty
and walked around his quarry.
One by one he saw their heads turning towards the ground.

Like a statue she stood gazing into the distance
in proud defiance of the shackles on her feet,
a queen resplendent on her throne.

He pulled the coarse blanket from her frame.
Her bare back glistened and her hands refused to search for modesty.
None among the twenty matched her pride.

Enraged he stripped away her loincloth,
a whip cracked and split the air then rose
to open wounds upon her flesh.

The tallest of the twenty stepped forward. Thirty pieces of silver
were scattered on the ground. He took the bill of sale,
placed his cloak upon her shoulders and unlocked her shackles.

She peered deep into his soul;
she saw a spirit released from bondage taking flight,
tasting the first sweetness of freedom's fine air.

134340

In 2006 scientists said Pluto
was no longer a real planet
and had to relinquish its name.
The celestial body became
binary dwarf planet 134340.

Not too fast, learned men and women of the skies.
We've known this little chap for a long time.
He's been part of the solar family since 1930.
Is this how you deal with unwanted relatives?

Is it because he is a bit slow? I know
Mercury circles the sun in 88 days
and sister Venus in 288, so I guess
Pluto's 247 years could get on your nerves.
But is speed everything?

How would you feel if you were demoted
and lost your name, retired and given
a number to remember yourself by?
Pick on someone your own size,
Jupiter or one of the other gas giants!

Have you no heart?
It's cold out there on the edge.
Sunlight takes six hours to arrive
and on a good day it is minus 230 degrees.
Someone's got to stand up for the small guy!

Silent Man

No it is a man said the mother to her child
whose arm and hand and small finger pointed
from the river bank
but he was here yesterday
and the day before said the mother
but why is he standing in the middle of the water?

Why does he not move?
hearing no reply a small hand squeezed tighter
a small head looked upwards to a mother's face
large eyes
silent and still
gazed upon the man
soft words floated out on the breeze

the child reached up and plucked them from the air
he's waiting
the waters of his world have been changeable of late
what was a modest flow increased
torrents raged and white
waters raced down
pushed forward through the narrow valleys.

Mercifully for a time all was quiet
but his promise of peace was broken
and wrath and vengeance rode upon the waves
for many hours he was almost submerged
many watched and feared
he would lose his footing
you can see even now it is far from calm.

Mother he just stares upstream
up the mountain
why don't you call out
louder
mother tell him we are here
tell him…
…there is no need my child
he knows he is not alone
once upon a time someone
somewhere held his hand.

Last Kick

Their sleek black bodies
glistened in the early morning light
they formed a circle around their victim
and with mechanical precision
delivered deathly blows.

The sound of my footsteps
disturb the frenzied feed
four black crows
scatter into flight
their beaks scarlet specked
cawing low deep accusing
demanding
their pound of flesh.

I kneel on the green grass
a young duckling seen here four weeks ago
glistening in a golden birthday suit
following its mother
father seeing off all who came too close.

Entrails have been dragged from its belly
eyes blinded
a still-soft beak wide open.

I witness a last kick
the final throb of a young heart
see a small life slowly slip away.

Touch the Earth

She was in control from the start
ran like a gazelle
taking each hurdle at her ease.
When others strained and moved ahead
her stride lengthened
effortlessly.

The beauty of her movement
mesmerised
as if she strode
upon the surface of a circling orb
and weights of lead
pulled all others down.

When the bell for the last lap sounded
she could have eased and ambled to the line.
Instead her head lifted.
Scenting a more glorious victory
she pushed on
her stride lengthening once again.

Like Icarus who flew and fell
the fall was mighty.
Sailing over the final hurdle
she lost her balance.

Force pushed her forward
gravity called her down.
For a moment she seemed beyond the grasp of nature
suspended
from strings of magic
in the hands of a master.

The air beneath her seemed like water
grateful to hold aloft such precious cargo,
her thighs spread wide
each powerful limb toned to perfection,
her long blonde hair stretched upwards
towards the heavens.

She hung like a puppet
the fingers of her left hand
centimetres above the red track
paused as if prepared to gently stroke
a precious piece of art.

Like a violin player
her right arm was raised
her wrist
angled
fingers
holding an invisible bow
in perfect poise.

Her face alone betrayed the pain.
Grazes and gashes
soon would heal.
In time to come
many laurels would rest upon her head.

I can never forget
the moment
never forget
the magnificence
of that mighty fall.

Altar Girl

If you can be one why can't I?
A girl can't be an altar boy he said
you're silly and counted out the marbles
and shook his head.

I don't see why I can't
I know all the Latin words
I can carry the water and the wine
and I can ring the bell.

She sat on the stone steps of the front door
and I can stay still longer than you
you fidget up there don't you?
she said and picked up her share of the marbles
and rolled them absent-mindedly
through her small fingers.

His eyes were on the ground
planning his next move
he did not see her look away
up in the clouds.

With her free hand she pointed
to the sky and with her finger
drew an outline in the air
a picture of her self

dressed in surplice and soutane
holding the small cruets
pouring the wine and a few water drops
smelling the incense

she listened to the sacred words
felt her own lips move
and best of best she rang the bell
to call the men and women of the world
to lift their eyes and look into the stars.

Feathers on the Breath of God

They came in silence

snowflakes in darkest night
raindrops in a beam of light
eyes filled with tender care
fragrance floating in the air
kisses past the midnight hour
eternal hope within a flower.

Feathers on the breath of God.

A Journey Through Time

My mother, my daughter and I are in the Japanese Gardens at Tully, County Kildare, Ireland. I grew up half an hour away. My daughter and I are visiting from Australia. Apart from the farm I was born on, some places in this country have remained dear to me. This one is top of the list. Returning today is like visiting an old friend, the sort you feel at home with when your eyes meet. Each moment is a pearl of great price: you know the face better than your own; your joy and gratitude are unmistakable; your eyes moisten as you receive in kind.

This place knows me well.

When we arrived and paid the entry fee, we were given the official brochure, which I had read many times. It has a map and a twenty-point description of the garden. The garden, which was completed in 1910, was designed to represent the course of human life from birth to death. Life begins at 'The Cave of Birth', represented as a cavern in a mound of rock. The small child has to pass along a dark tunnel. This is called 'The Tunnel of Ignorance'. The child is deemed to lack the light of understanding. As he gets older he moves along and up the steps of 'The Hill of Learning'. The challenges of teenage years and adolescence are negotiated and he arrives at the edge of adulthood. This stage of life is a junction, called 'The Parting of the Ways'. A fundamental choice is to be made: a carefree existence can be chosen, depicted by a smooth pathway; a narrow and restricted life of living alone; the more adventurous and risky option of entry into a relationship of marriage.

The remainder of the garden will describe the life events of those who choose the latter course. Seeking love takes one to

'The Island of Joy and Wonder', 'The Engagement Bridge' and onwards to 'The Marriage Bridge' and 'The Honeymoon Path'.

The struggles and challenges are represented by steep paths and dead ends. This part of the garden is higher. You can see where you have come from and have a better view of the future. 'The Hill of Ambition' depicts hopes and ideals. Failures are represented by the cul-de-sac of 'Disappointment'.

The declining years of life are suggested by the walk down from the hill. Two stone gods sit on either side of the waterfall, and suggest the need for prayer, gratitude and guidance.

The walk is now easy. The 'Teahouse' provides a place to linger. A visit to 'The Well of Wisdom' suggests the need for enlightenment. A small space called the garden of 'Peace and Contentment' is nearby and access is by a red bridge, 'The Bridge of Life'.

Simplicity characterises this part. 'The Chair of Old Age' depicts taking one's ease. 'The Hill of Mourning', a slight incline in the corner of the garden, surrounded by weeping trees, is the place where one's life-force is relinquished.

One leaves the garden by 'The Gateway to Eternity', just as one had entered by the gate on the other side, 'The Gate of Oblivion'. The human spirit or soul is in a state of transition or pilgrimage. It entered the human body at birth, and now passes into eternity.

Knowing all this as we enter through 'The Gate of Oblivion', I prefer to let the philosophy slide to the back of my mind. A youthful Japanese maple is the first to greet us. It is no more than knee high, a delicate shade of pink, and has all the open freshness of childhood. I wonder what its future holds.

The honest fragrance of the newly mown grass presents

itself and I await further indulgence. The cool air of 'The Cave of Birth' is followed by the accepting warmth of the sun. As I move about I like to half close my eyes and allow the colours of the place to dance before me. Yellows, reds, pinks, browns and blues, and the forty shades of Irish green, flow in and out and through each other.

The bees silently go about their work; where water can be heard, it flows with cleansing clearness. I pick up and carry in the palm of my hand a freshly fallen blossom and a rose petal; then later lay them gently upon a much-weathered rock. The redness of 'The Bridge of Life' reflects in the still water below.

We move around, coming together and going away again. Brief words pass between us.

I was last here four years ago. Some trees have grown tall, and the bonsais are to be congratulated on a few centimetres' advance.

The sundial and the corkscrew hazel, *Corglus Avellaur Contorta*, seem to have stood still and awaited my return. It is now summer and my last two visits were in spring and autumn. Seasonal changes blend in my mind. Past, present and future are united.

My mother, my daughter and I have gravitated to the garden seat. We sit with our backs to the high wall. Silence has come down. Earlier, people and their cameras were everywhere. 'Closer. No, not to me, together!' 'Careful, we don't want you falling into "The Well of Wisdom".' Laughter.

Other fragments of conversations drifted before us and were gone. When we sat some offered a polite 'Hello' or 'Nice day'. Later, half-smiles knew we needed to be left alone. Then the place was empty. Even the full-throated chatter of the birds ceased.

They had flown away into the adjoining garden. And now, the strange quietness which follows sound, descends. The dappled sunbeams dance gently on our faces: the air tingles; the willows shimmer; everything holds its breath.

Like the small flat stone sent skimming across the surface of a lake, the number four skims across my mind. I am about to let it sink, and search for something sensible, but I let it play on. A sequence presents itself.

It is 2004. The original garden was completed ninety-four years ago and took four years to build. Our ages all end in four, eighty-four, fifty-four, and fourteen. Perhaps the mind at play is not so silly after all!

In a far corner of the garden a man empties a wheelbarrow on a compost heap. Its contents, fragments of his morning's work, stand in a newly formed pile. Something in me is released. I let time dissolve. From all corners of the life which I have shared with these two people, from all points on the compass of our history, fragments of the past awake and tumble forth.

I look at 'The Bridge of Life' and see my daughter twelve years ago as a toddler, under the watchful eye of her mother, making her uncertain way over the wooden structure. She turns and reappears as a confident six-year-old, authoritatively instructing her brother – who has ascended to the two-year-old-place in the family – on how to direct his life, or at least his feet. Torn between the getting of wisdom and feeding the mallard he has spotted in the stream, he opts for the latter. Her sententious mood lightens, and soon she is of the opinion the duck is the better bet, and echoes her brother's call for bread. 'Dad?' 'Dad?'

Now fourteen, she sits beside me. Is she remembering herself all those years ago? I move my eyes – without turning my head

– and steal a glance at the side of her face. Her eye has a sparkle; her mouth is open and happy. I chuckle at the light in her face. Meanwhile, old habits die hard and my fingers move about in my pocket, searching for crusts.

My mother sits as still as a statue. I want to ask her when she first came here. But words, like birds, have flown away. Here, and now, silence and memory reign.

I wonder what memories have come alive for her. I know she was here with us when our son and our daughter were two, absorbing all the comings and goings with girlish glee. When we passed through the town of her birth, half an hour ago, we drove by the cemetery where her mother was laid in the earth.

My grandmother died when my mother was two; no mother to watch over her as she made her uncertain way across the bridges of life. Who taught her what she is doing now?

I steal a sidewards glance at her. She is like my daughter: her mouth slightly open; her heart receiving the world around her. Forty years melt away. I am fourteen lying in my bed at home, preparing for sleep. It is July – this time of year – and the evenings are long. My mother comes in and stands sideways, beside the window. The setting sun is behind her. She is in contemplative mood.

She would often make her appearance in this way. She would stand and talk. As she wandered into the room, so also she would wander into her past. She told stories. I listened. Her silhouette will remain with me forever. Her words painted pictures and I could 'see' everything she spoke of. I can still remember the hours she spent, when she was twenty-two, on a railway station in England, waiting for a connection to take her to Leeds, where she had found work as a nurse during the Second World War.

The atmosphere she conjured up, speaking softly, naturally, all the time standing sideways, was so real I felt I had been on the railway station watching her – a young woman taking new steps in the world. Now with our backs to the high wall, I look at her again. For the first time it dawns on me why she did it.

She looked sideways because she was 'seeing' it all again. She was back there, living through it. She can be two, twenty-two and eighty-four at the same time. The roots of her life did not break at a tender age, but in adversity found others to grow with and expand. Now, in the sunset of her life, she returns to her well-stored past for the rich pickings.

I steal a glance into the future and 'see' my daughter aged twenty-two, taking new steps in the world. My pride and joy; my hope surpassed. She has sat with us for twenty minutes and no words have been called for. She too can sit as still as a living statue. Such receptive silence speaks peace with one's self.

I see a robin, hopping, faintly chirping, and slowly my ears attune to a distant chorus, announcing the return of the chattering birds and, perhaps, the next wave of visitors. It must be time to go.

I hesitate. My mother's silhouette, and the countless times I saw it, returns and skims across the surface of my mind. I have carried these memories with me for forty years or more – I have waited until today for new light to fall upon them. Perhaps they're like the paintings on the stairways of our lives: we have passed them every day; we are always on the go; we are yet to stop and stare. Patiently, they wait; their speech will be in silence.

The spirit of this place knows me well. Today it has delved deep within me. I am replenished. I see all these memories as fine, ethereal substances. If we fix our gaze hard on them, they become rough-hewn and coarse. If our sight awaits them in the middle distance, they dance nimbly before our eyes.

Such delicate translucent objects, such priceless pearls, require careful handling, like petal and blossom carried in the palm of the hand. The three generations will soon have walked out of the garden through the door which symbolises 'The Gateway to Eternity'. Where will our lives have taken us when we come again in four more years?

For now, may we all rest in silent peace.

Like a bird flying past the window

'Like a bird flying past the window
that's how your life goes by.'
He spoke these words to the young mother
she with her brood of four
he a bachelor
on the edge of his three score years and ten
both observing the setting sun
each being observed.

He lived alone
his small thatched cottage
leaning on the side of the farmhouse
his dogs lapped milk from a sunken flagstone
'No distemper here,' he used to say
he had a dresser and he slept in a settle-bed,
opened up and laid down each night
and folded up each morning
I never saw it open though I often sat on it
watched the turf fire
and the toast he made tasted of the bog
sweet with a plentiful supply of country butter
pure gold.

Mrs Dale's Diary, the recording of the daily
happenings in the life of a doctor's family
every day religiously at a quarter past four
my mother turned on the wireless
at a quarter past four Danny's door closed
he knelt with his back to the fire, saying the rosary
his elbows resting on the large armchair
like a church pew.

At half past four everyone returned to their world
four more children came
there were bicycle punctures to be mended
calves and chickens to be fed
knives to be sharpened.

He died forty-five years ago
a bird flew past my window today
that's how my life goes by.

Small Beginnings

It was the hardest thing I did in my life
cracked my heart in two you said
leave four small children at the gate
turn and step into the old black Ford.

I can travel with you now
I sit beside the brown suitcase in the back seat
torrents of tears flowing your gaunt face promising
one day you will return to us.

Two years of our lives you lost
an iron will steered you back
complete with an ocean of love
that kissed the shores of all our lives for all our days.

Soon I will be twice the age you were when you departed
Now I am the tallest of them all
then the smallest
and part of me stands
still at the gate
one hand inside my trousers pocket
the other in a brother's hand
the old black Ford splutters into life
moves through the avenue of beech trees
disappears behind the high hedge
falls over the edge of the earth.

Old Cow

'You what? You ate those beans?'
My mother drops her eyes in the full force
of my brother's gentle chiding.
'They're cattle feed,' he added swiftly, smiled
and waited. I watch the gentle tease enjoy the wait
as much as any answer the joust is always
the same always full of surprises.
'Does this mean,' she said, her short shrill
laugh like a referee's whistle resumes
the play, 'I'll turn into a cow?'
'Come to think of it,' she added warming to the
challenge, 'there are certain advantages.
Four legs are better than two. When these old pins
are tired' – and here she folds her arms
adopts a Buddha pose – 'I can chew the cud
and give the front two a rest. How about that?'

Maternal Light

Hand me a canvas and I will mark your outline
standing beside the bedroom window

I stared at the ceiling as the night began
to drain the light from the day

your sign to step into the shape you made
the night before and the night before that

and always when I turn and lean on my elbow
I see you smile as you stare into your past your time

in Leeds and Bradford during the war the small suitcase
packed under the bed ready to leave

at a moment's notice when the siren sounds
a siren has now swept you away forever

your outline remains but the space inside
is emptied of all light and of all grace

and never again will you fill the place we shared
the space that held the fabric of my dreams

Shades of Life

I see it clear as summer morning sunlight
streaming through the open windows of my adult years.
I see the fields of Shangana in all their seasons:
the freshly turned brown earth of spring
the rising green shoots of summer
the golden barley swaying in the autumn breeze
the cold wet earth of the year's grey end.

I look into the face of each of you my children
and in your eyes I see writ large
chronicles of lives lived and living
I see the peace and pain
that is the lot of each and every life
of yours and mine
inside my fragile mind there dwells a vast ocean
of memory
that all the streams of years
of time and place have filled.

Last night when I was sleeping
a storm passed by
trees were felled
the Barrow burst its banks
the outer regions of my thoughts were all submerged.

Pity me then
but I forbid you to make me an object of your pity
I have lived a life of which I am justly proud
and if you are at a loss with me
remember this
all you need to know already has been learned.

Remember my child when you were a babe
I sat with you and in silence held your hand
your face
your eyes
words and thoughts
and the great span of life
were beyond us
a father and husband kept watch
all that was required
was the peace and the presence of each other.

So
remember
the kingdom of love is within you
and as my life was consecrated to your dreams
draw close as my day draws to its close
do not despair
be sad
rejoice in the life I have lived
guard what I have given you
do not fret after tomorrow
the precious moment we now share
is elegantly sufficient
forever
let me live forever
in the buoyant sea
of your life's remembrance.

Old Friends

For B.W. & M.G.

The heavy iron gate clipped shut
and the dark wooden door opened
they stepped forward and faced each other
across the yard
together they have lived one hundred and seventy-six years
in the space between
a friendship
that was a mainstay in their lives.

Uncertain steps send sounds of hope
a fragile mind has made the ground uneven
hearts quicken
aged hands reach out
aged foreheads bend and touch.

Each stands
            like a butterfly poised upon a flower,
            like a flying buttress holding erect a sacred structure.

In a moment talk will fill the air
like the briefest scent of the sweetest rose
like a sun gleam visiting a rain drop
this moment will pass
and will be recorded forever
in the annals of their lives.

Shades of Death

The summit belonged to my guide
and she stood with it within her command,
arms outstretched like a figure on a cross.
She faced me then looked away.
Her left arm lowered and my eyes followed
her right hand towards the east.
'What you see,' she said, 'came slowly upon us
the daily grind of millions of earth years
small increments and depletions
the work of wind and water, earth and fire.'

She turned to face the west.
The left side of her cross rose, the other lowered.
'There,' she said, 'we have an altogether different picture.
There the ground split and the surface plates collided.
If the eyes of man or woman had existed
huge boulders would have been seen blown to dust and ash.
Now of course' – her cross had disappeared and she stood
and faced me once again – 'it's hard to tell the difference.
The great forces of nature have tempered all. On the surface
they are the same. To understand we dig deep.'

What incidence of nature took control and shaped the
contours of your life? With my guide and me alas it was
not peaceful. To tell the truth it started that way,
with peace I mean and I can know within me
the gentle flow of water upon the pebbled river bed,
the warm caress of the hand upon my smiling face,
the touch of lips of tender peace.

Then, in the twinkling of an eye she was gone.
Her body failed and she departed and fear filled
the shadows of her faltering steps. Somehow I survived.
I don't know how. I can't recall. Another, older witness
said he saw a small boy bewildered and bereft. When I
look at him I see another hand reaching high to open
her bedroom door another face finding her bed empty
another voice howling at the vacant room.

This story is like an older brother's clothes, a hand-me-down.
All I know is the emptiness within. I stand upon the summit
of my world, naked, bereft of words. The scaffolding that holds
and binds my frame is threatened with extinction. A single
false move and I will be blown away to dust and ashes.

Earth wind and water and last of all fire
hardest to come by but necessary in the hour
of greatest need, the smouldering heat that seeks out justice,
the red-hot flame that hankers for revenge,
the blind and naked hatred that grows when pain and suffering
cast their shadows on one of young and tender years.
In the interests of safety and some higher goal
these forces within have always been corralled.

She came back some time later two earth years later,
an eternity in a child's time and now half a century on
she is preparing to depart again, this time for good.
I am fifty-five years older and fifty-five years wiser
than I was then but who can tell what this new disappearance
will foster in its wake what elemental forces will be unleashed
what earth and water and wind and fire will break lose
what littleness what emptiness will be shown to all the world.

Adieu

my land shuddered
tectonic plates
still
since the beginning
of my time
moved

your body
that part of mother
earth
that gave me life
I lower
into the ground

Unspoken Remains

words fall
like flakes of snow
onto my eyes
mingle in the stream
of questions

questions stream
from the tops of
mountains
race towards the sea
searching

searching for your
mind's wide ocean
slowed by the searing sun
they trickle into the cracks
of the parched river bed

Return

With thanks to Thomas Hardy

When you spoke to me last evening
turned your head
paused and looked away
as if the space I occupied had been vacated
and you talked on as if you were talking to yourself
why did you not wait
for an answer?

When you listened to the rustle
of the leaves in the trees
and when you bent low
and drank the fragrance of the ripe red rose
and when you pointed to the meadow
and said it quivered in the wind
like the surface of the sea
you spoke and called my name
and smiled that smile I have known
since the day you were born
why did you not wait
for an answer?

Two weeks past when thunder shook the night
and lightening painted the room silver-white
you sat on your hands and you stared at the rain
trickle down the window pane
you rocked to and fro and paused
poised to reach for my hand
why did your body say no
why did it not wait
for an answer?

Listen
listen to the wind
it kisses the leaves like my lips
kissed your forehead
the day you were born
and now morning comes
a morning free from blemish
the fragrance of a new day
rising.

Close your eyes and you will see me
hear your heart beat and you will feel me
breathe quietly and you will touch me
listen beyond the silence and you will hear me
and you won't have to wait
for an answer.

High Flyer 2

Soaring on wings
high above the escarpment
circling

while the hour-glass builds
a small mountain
of sand

time to turn back
time to be guided
to float in large circles

welcome
the end of all movement
the end of all time.

Ingram Content Group UK Ltd.
Milton Keynes UK
UKHW020107090323
418239UK00014B/1036